MW00890301

To:

_____

From:

_____

The Story of Noah and the Ark

THE BIG FLOOD

Written and Illustrated by Paul & Delores Gully

BroadStreet
KIDS

Published by BroadStreet Kids
BroadStreet Kids is an imprint of

BroadStreet Publishing® Group, LLC
Savage, Minnesota USA
BroadStreetPublishing.com

The Big Flood: The Story of Noah and the Ark

Written and illustrated by Paul & Delores Gully

Copyright © 2018 Paul & Delores Gully

ISBN 978-1-4245-5640-3 (hardcover)
ISBN 978-1-4245-5721-9 (ebook)

All rights reserved. No part of this book may be reproduced in any form, except for brief quotations in printed reviews, without permission in writing from the publisher.

Stock or custom editions of BroadStreet Publishing titles may be purchased in bulk for educational, business, ministry, fundraising, or sales promotional use. For information, please e-mail info@broadstreetpublishing.com.

Printed in China

18 19 20 21   5 4 3 2 1

This true story
is from
Genesis 5:32–10:1
in the Bible.

God loved a man named Noah,
and Noah loved God too.
God had big plans for Noah.
What do you think he'll do?

God commanded Noah
to build a massive boat.
"I'm sending lots of rain.
You will need to float."

Everyone else was wicked.
They mocked the good and pure.
They'd never heard of rain.
"Impossible! We're sure."

Noah had three sons
who helped him build each day.
For over fifty years,
they didn't get to play.

Noah begged the people,
"Repent and change your ways.
There's room on board for all
who love the God that saves."

Then God called to the animals
and brought them two by two.
Noah told his family,
"Our boat is now a zoo."

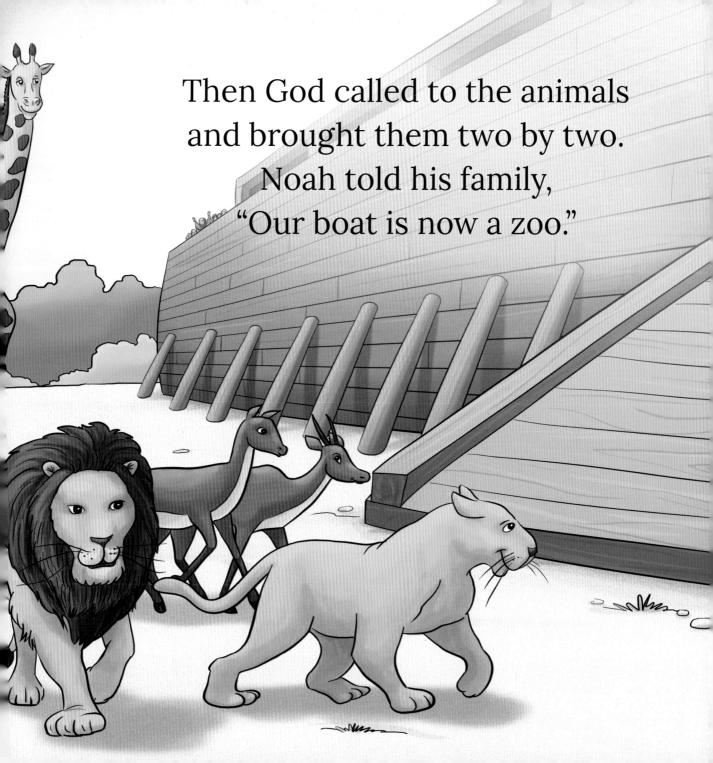

On the ark they went,
each to find their stall.
From elephants to mice,
there was room for all.

When everything was ready,
God came and shut the door.
Drip, drip, drop!

The rain began to pour.

For forty days and nights,
rain fell from the sky.
Outside the waves were rising.
Inside was safe and dry.

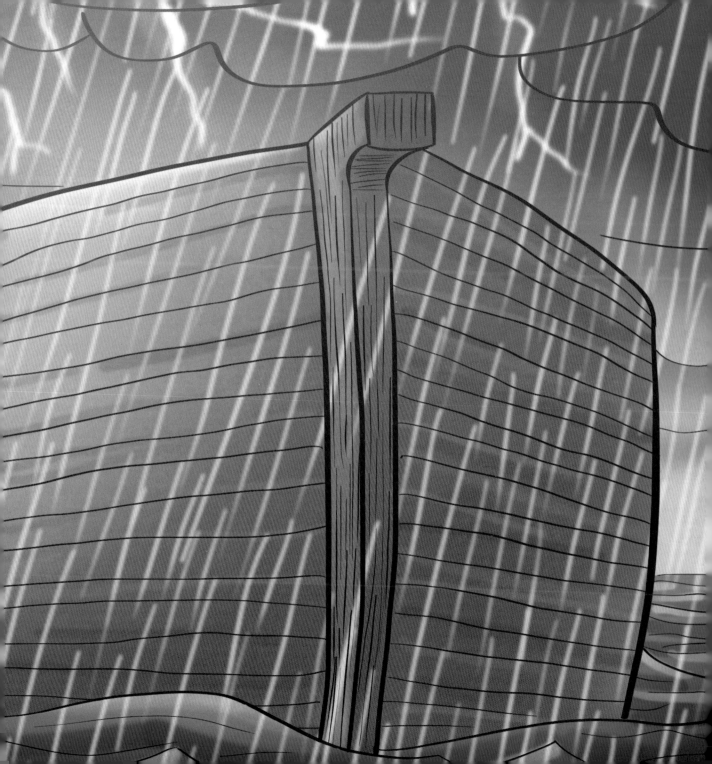

Taking care of animals
was not an easy chore.
God remembered Noah,
and then it rained no more.

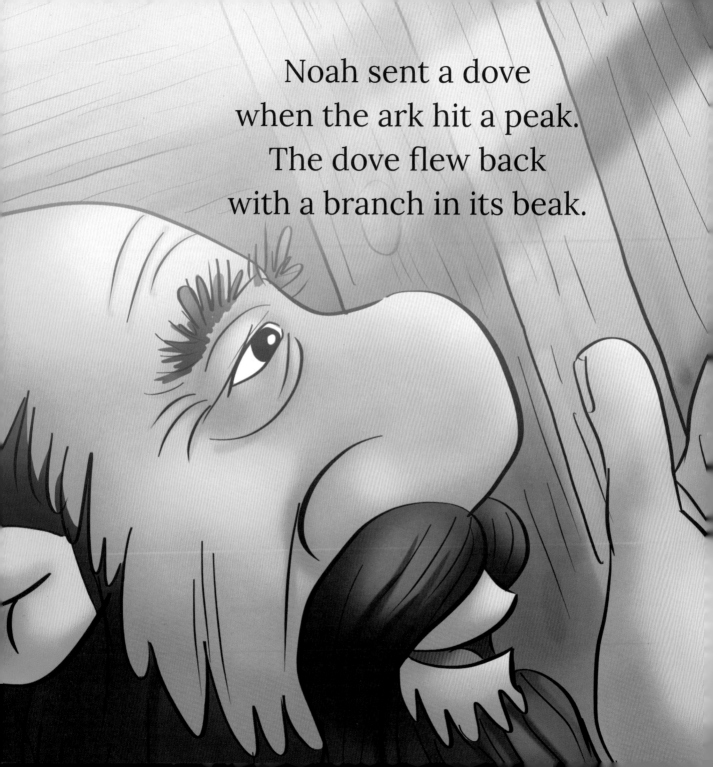

Noah sent a dove
when the ark hit a peak.
The dove flew back
with a branch in its beak.

After many days,
the ground was finally dry.
Then everyone came out,
and praises filled the sky!

God painted the first rainbow—
a promise for all to see.
He'll never flood the earth again.
He loves us: You and Me.

When God gives you a job
you may not understand,
you can always trust him,
and follow his big plan.

If you'd like to know God's plan for
your life and be his special child,
say this simple prayer to God called

The ABC Prayer.

 ADMIT:
Admit that you are a sinner.
(That means you have done wrong things.)

 BELIEVE:
Believe that Jesus is God's only Son, and he chose to
die on a cross for the wrong things you've done.

 COMMIT:
Commit to Jesus as Lord
(that means he is first place in your life),
and confess that to others
(confess means to tell people).

God loved

so much that he gave
his only Son, so that if

believes in him,

will not die, but

will have life forever.

JOHN 3:16

WRITE YOUR NAME IN THE SPACES OF THIS BIBLE VERSE

Paul and Delores Gully currently reside in the mountains of Dillard, Georgia. They met while attending Ringling College of Art and Design where Delores mistook Paul for one of his identical triplet brothers, who was in her class. Their God-given talent has been utilized to illustrate books and curriculum worldwide. Their passion is to help children understand how much God loves them. They enjoy traveling, hiking, fishing, reading, bicycling, and watching action movies.

Connect with the Gullys at PaulGullyIllustrator.com and Facebook.com/pvggraphicsanddesign.

Enjoy another great Bible story!

A *Giant Headache* is the biblical story of David and Goliath in a rhyming, fun format. It teaches how we receive courage and strength from God when we trust in him completely.

The soldiers all line up.
A battle will begin.
Who will be the bravest?
Who is going to win?

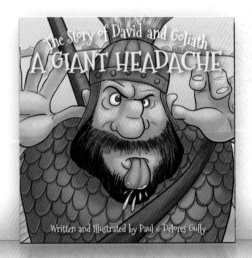